Differentiated Instruction

Instructional and Management Tools to Help Every Child Succeed

Macmillan/McGraw-Hill

Differentiated Instruction

Differentiated instruction fosters successful learning by adapting instruction to meet students' needs. Differentiated instruction means:

- Modifying teaching to accommodate students' needs and performance.
- Implementing data-informed whole group and small group instruction.
- Using leveled reading materials to provide successful reading experiences.

How Does Treasures Support Differentiated Instruction?

Macmillan/McGraw-Hill *Treasures* provides leveled instructional materials and a management system for successfully implementing differentiated instruction.

- Use whole group lessons to introduce, model, teach, and review skills and concepts.
- Use **Teacher-Led Small Groups** to differentiate the instruction presented in whole group.
- Use **Cross-Curricular Workstations** to provide activities that reinforce key skills and concepts.
- Use **Independent Activities** to provide meaningful practice.

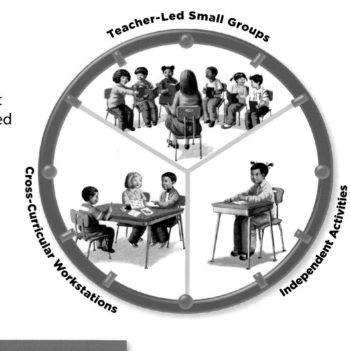

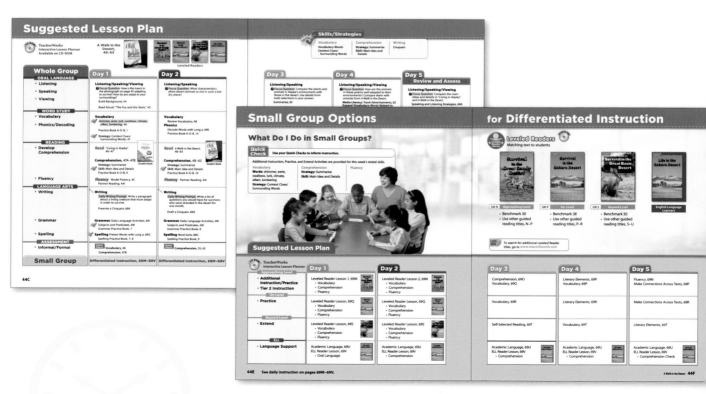

What Do I Teach in Small Groups?

Small group lessons provide targeted skills instruction. The lessons are structured so that students respond frequently, allowing teachers to monitor responses and modify instruction as needed.

Quick Checks are used as informal observations during whole group instruction to determine what additional instruction students need. This data helps inform teachers what to teach in small groups.

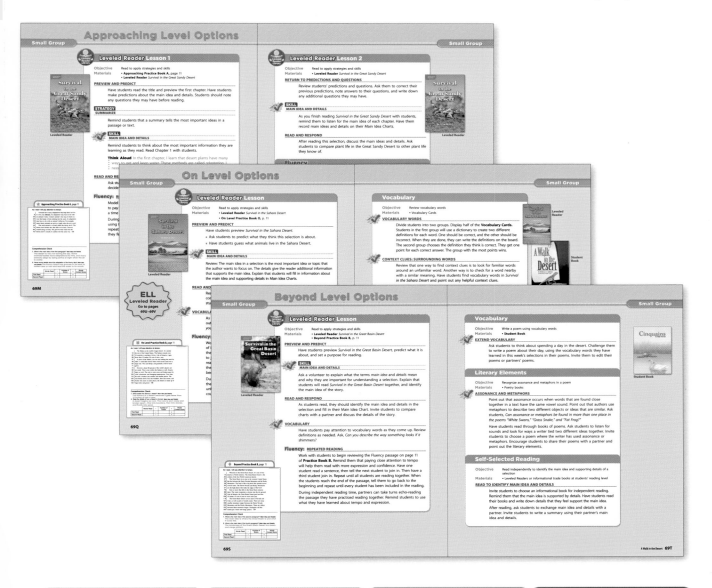

Approaching Level	On Level	Beyond Level	English Language Learners
• Provides additional instruction and practice • For students who have some difficulty with skills	• Offers opportunities to practice and reinforce grade-level skills • For students who understand skills, but need additional practice	• Provides suggestions for extending skills and concepts • For students who have mastered the skill	• Suggestions for modifying instruction for English Language Learners • An ELL lesson to develop Academic Language and support ELL Readers

What Do I Teach in Small Groups?

Macmillan/McGraw-Hill Leveled Readers incorporate the same key concept, skills, and vocabulary taught during whole group instruction.

Approaching Level

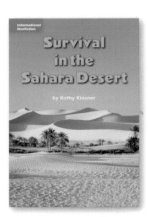

On Level

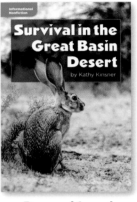

Beyond Level

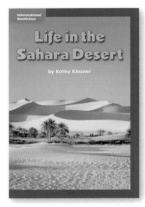

English Language Learners

What Do I Do with the Rest of the Class?

Independent Practice

Treasures provides components that allow students to independently practice and apply key skills and concepts taught in whole group and small group instruction.

Literacy Activities for writing and cross-curricular connections

Leveled Practice Workbooks for practicing key skills

Cross-Curricular Workstation Activities

Students of mixed abilities extend learning in small study groups at the workstations. They are encouraged to work together to enhance understanding.

Provides additional suggestions for Workstations, including Dinah Zike's Foldables™

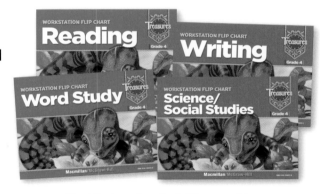

The Workstation Activities provide opportunities for:

- Independent Reading
- Independent Writing
- Fluency Practice
- Building Words and Vocabulary
- Cross-Curricular Activities
- Technology

How Do I Make Data-Driven Decisions?

Quick Checks

Quick Checks in the Teacher's Edition lessons remind teachers to check for understanding of a skill or concept. This data helps to plan instruction, group students, and select materials appropriate for instruction and practice.

Weekly and Unit Assessments

Weekly and Unit Assessments are more formal tools for monitoring progress and for making grouping decisions.

What Tools Can I Use for Time Management?

Weekly Student Contracts

Weekly contracts help organize and prioritize tasks for students. They let students know what assignments to complete throughout the week.

As work is completed, assignments can be stored with the contract in a folder. Folders can be sent home for family members to review.

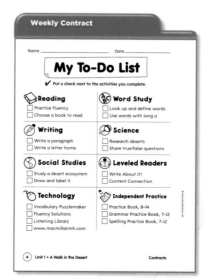